The
BAPTISM BOOK

Rite of Infant Baptism

The Rite of Baptism during Mass
The Rite of Baptism for One Child
The Rite of Baptism for
Several Children

A Redemptorist Publication

The **BAPTISM BOOK**
Published by
Redemptorist Publications

Editor: Francis Dickinson, C.SS.R.
This compilation © 1975 Redemptorist Publications
A Registered Charity limited by guarantee.
Registered in England 3261721

Fifty eighth printing   December 2000 (287th thousand)

English translation of the rite of baptism for children
Copyright © 1969 International Committee on English on the Liturgy
Inc. All rights reserved.

Translation confirmed by the Sacred Congregation of Divine Worship,
15th April 1970 (Prot. N. 1667/70)

Scripture texts from the Jerusalem Bible © 1966 by Darton, Longman
and Todd Ltd., and Doubleday & Co. Inc. and used by permission.

        Concordat cum originali:
        Fr John Dewis
        10th May 1975

Approved for Liturgical use in Scotland.
Joseph V. Boyd (Secretary to Scottish National Liturgical Commission)
6th June 1975

ISBN 0 85231 164 8

Printed by Coltec Parker Limited Keighley BD21 3LG

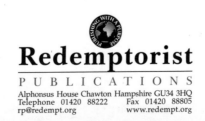

Redemptorist
P U B L I C A T I O N S
Alphonsus House Chawton Hampshire GU34 3HQ
Telephone 01420 88222   Fax 01420 88805
rp@redempt.org   www.redempt.org

Using this book ...

You will find this book easy to follow. If baptism is taking place during Sunday Mass, start at page 4. Otherwise, if yours is the only child being baptized start at page 8; if other children are also being baptized, turn first to page 19.

Parents and Godparents

The most striking feature of this new rite of baptism is the part parents play in it. They present their children for baptism ; they renew their own faith ; they solemnly accept the responsibility of training their child in the Catholic Faith. This does not mean that godparents have been replaced, but their role is a more realistic one of assisting parents in the religious upbringing of their children, particularly by good example.

a Non-Catholic Parent

The new rite of baptism presumes that both parents are Catholics. A non-Catholic parent is asked to join in the prayers and responses only in so far as he, or she, feels able. Don't fear you will embarrass anybody if there are times when you remain silent. All, and especially the priest, will understand.

How to act

Finally, nobody need worry about where to stand or where to move during the service. These details are now left very much to the priest so that he may arrange them in the way best suited to the design of his Church. Let him be your guide.

The Rite of Baptism during Mass

During the baptismal part of the rite (as indicated below), the mother, rather than the godparents, holds the child. If the child has a white garment (shawl), this should be left aside until the appropriate moment of the rite.

Introductory Rites

The Mass is that of the Sunday. The Entry Antiphon is said or sung, or a suitable hymn sung, as the Priest approaches the altar.

Priest: In the name of the Father, and of the Son, and of the Holy Spirit.

All: **Amen.**

The Priest may announce the theme of the Mass.

RECEPTION OF THE CHILDREN

The Priest questions the Parents of each child in these or similar words:

Priest: What name have you given your child?
The Parents give the child's name.

Priest: What do you ask of God's Church for N.?
Parents: **Baptism.**

The Priest addresses all the Parents together:

Priest: You have asked to have your children (child) baptised. In doing so you are accepting the responsibility of training them (him, her) in the practice of the faith. It will be your duty to bring them (him, her) up to keep God's commandments as Christ taught us, by loving God and our neighbour. Do you clearly understand what you are undertaking?
Parents: **We do.**

4

The Priest next addresses the Godparents:

Priest: Are you ready to help these parents in their duty as Christian mothers and fathers?

Godparents: **We are.**

Addressing the Children to be baptized:

Priest: My dear children,

(if only one child he greets it by name)

the Christian community welcomes you with great joy. In its name I claim you for Christ our Saviour by the sign of his cross. I now trace the cross on your forehead(s), and invite your parents (and godparents) to do the same.

He signs each child on the forehead and invites parents and godparents to do the same.

GLORIA

The Gloria is now said or sung, except in Advent and Lent.

Priest: Glory to God in the highest,
All: **and peace to his people on earth.**
Lord God, heavenly King,
almighty God and Father,
we worship you, we give you thanks,
we praise you for your glory.

Lord Jesus Christ, only Son of the Father,
Lord God, Lamb of God,
you take away the sin of the world:
have mercy on us:
you are seated at the right hand of the Father:
receive our prayer.

For you alone are the Holy One,
you alone are the Lord,
you alone are the Most High,
Jesus Christ,
with the Holy Spirit,
in the glory of God the Father. Amen.

COLLECT

Priest Let us pray.

There is a short pause for silent prayer, after which the Priest says, or sings, the Collect, to which the people answer:

All: **Amen.**

Liturgy of the Word

THE FIRST READING

All sit and listen to the First Reading, at the end of which the Reader says:

R: This is the Word of the Lord.
C: **Thanks be to God.**

RESPONSORIAL PSALM

The Reader announces the Response. The Congregation repeats it after him, and repeats it again after each verse of the Psalm.

THE SECOND READING

On Sundays and some other days there is a Second Reading, at the end of which the Reader says:

    This is the Word of the Lord.
All: **Thanks be to God.**

ALLELUIA

The Alleluia or Acclamation is now sung: otherwise it may be said or omitted. The Congregation stands.

THE GOSPEL

Before reading the Gospel the Priest prays quietly:

Priest: Almighty God, cleanse my heart and my lips
            that I may worthily proclaim your gospel.

            Aloud, he says:
Priest: The Lord be with you.
All: **And also with you.**
Priest: A reading from the holy gospel according to N.
All: **Glory to you, Lord.**

            At the end of the reading he says:
Priest: This is the gospel of the Lord.
All: **Praise to you, Lord Jesus Christ.**

            Quietly, as he kisses the book:
Priest: May the words of the gospel wipe away our sins.

THE SERMON

A Homily is now given, but the Creed which usually follows it is omitted, because a profession of faith will be made by all during the baptismal rite.

THE BIDDING PRAYER

The Bidding Prayers (page 10 or 21) are now said, to which extra invocations may be added for the needs of the Church and the world.

BAPTISM

The celebration of Baptism continues with the Prayer of Exorcism, Anointing, and other ceremonies, as given on pages 12-16 and 23-27.

THE MASS

After the Celebration of Baptism, the Mass continues in the usual way with the Offertory.

FINAL BLESSING

The blessing at the end of Mass may be that which concludes the Baptism Rite (page 17 or 28).

The Rite of Baptism for One Child

Throughout the ceremony, except where indicated otherwise, the mother (rather than the godparents) holds the child. If the child has a white baptismal garment (shawl), this should be left aside until the appropriate moment in the rite.

Reception of the Child

A suitable hymn or psalm may be sung by the people.

The Priest greets the Parents, Godparents and Friends at the church door (or wherever is customary) and speaks to them of the special joy of this occasion.

He then questions the Parents in these or similar words:

Priest: What name have you given your child?
          The Parents give the child's name.

Priest: What do you ask of God's Church for N.?
Parents: **Baptism.**

Priest: You have asked to have your child baptized. In doing so you are accepting the responsibility of training him (her) in the practice of the faith. It will be your duty to bring him (her) up to keep God's commandments as Christ taught us, by loving God and our neighbour. Do you clearly understand what you are undertaking?
Parents: **We do.**

The Priest now addresses the Godparents as follows:

Priest: Are you ready to help the parents of this child in their duty as Christian parents?

Godparents: **We are.**

The Priest says to the Child:

Priest: N., the Christian community welcomes you with great joy. In its name I claim you for Christ our Saviour by the sign of his cross. I now trace the cross on your forehead, and invite your parents (and godparents) to do the same.

He signs the child on the forehead and invites parents and godparents to do the same.

All now proceed to the place where the Celebration of God's Word will be held. If the baby is restless it may be taken outside during this next part of the ceremony, but the parents and godparents should be present.

Celebration of God's Word

READINGS

One or more gospel passages are read (texts p. 32) to which all listen attentively. These tell us of what God has revealed to us about baptism, and of the new life, a share in God's life, that is to be given to the child. (Texts for a fuller Celebration of the Word are given on pp 30-32).

HOMILY

A short Homily or Instruction is now given (at the end of which the Priest may invite those present to pray silently for a short time).

THE BIDDING PRAYER

The Intercessions follow, with these or similar invocations:

Priest: My dear brethren, let us ask our Lord Jesus Christ to look lovingly on this child who is to be baptized, on his (her) parents and godparents and on all the baptized.

Reader: By the mystery of your death and resurrection, bathe this child in light, give him (her) the new life of baptism and welcome him (her) into your holy Church.
Lord, hear us.

All: **Lord, graciously hear us.**

Reader: Through baptism and confirmation, make him (her) your faithful follower and a witness to your gospel.
Lord, hear us.

All: **Lord, graciously hear us.**

Reader: Lead him (her) by a holy life to the joys of God's Kingdom.
Lord, hear us.

All: **Lord, graciously hear us.**

Reader: Make the lives of his (her) parents and godparents examples of faith to inspire this child.
Lord, hear us.

All: **Lord, graciously hear us.**

Reader:	Keep his (her) family always in your love.
	Lord, hear us.
All:	**Lord, graciously hear us.**

Reader:	Renew the grace of our baptism in each one of us.
	Lord, hear us.
All:	**Lord, graciously hear us.**

If the child was taken out earlier, it is now brought back again.

INVOCATION OF THE SAINTS

The Priest leads the Invocation of the Saints, as follows:

| Priest: | Holy Mary, Mother of God, |
| All: | **Pray for us.** |

| Priest: | Saint John the Baptist, |
| All: | **Pray for us.** |

| Priest: | Saint Joseph, |
| All: | **Pray for us.** |

| Priest: | Saint Peter and Saint Paul, |
| All: | **Pray for us.** |

| Priest: | Saint N |

He may here add the names of other patron saints, e.g. those of the child, of the church and of the place. To each, the People answer:

| All: | **Pray for us.** |

| Priest: | All holy men and women. |
| All: | **Pray for us.** |

Exorcism and Anointing

PRAYER OF EXORCISM

The Prayer of Exorcism (of which the following is one form), and the Anointing with Oil of Catechumens, prepare the child for the coming of the new life of God in baptism.

Priest: Almighty and ever-living God,
you sent your only Son into the world
to cast out the power of Satan, spirit of evil,
to rescue man from the kingdom of darkness,
and bring him into the splendour of your kingdom
     of light.
We pray for this child:
set him (her) free from original sin,
make him (her) a temple of your glory,
and send your Holy Spirit to dwell with him (her).
Through Christ our Lord.

All: **Amen.**

ANOINTING

Priest: We anoint you with the oil of salvation
in the name of Christ our Saviour:
may he strengthen you
with his power,
who lives and reigns for ever and ever.

All: **Amen.**

The Priest anoints the child on the breast with the Oil of Catechumens, to strengthen it with the power of Christ.

PROCESSION

All now proceed to the baptistery.

Celebration of the Sacrament

At the font the Priest reminds those present of the wonderful work of God whose plan it is to sanctify man, body and soul, through water. He may use these or similar words:

Priest: My dear brethren, God uses the sacrament of water to give his divine life to those who believe in him. Let us turn to him, and ask him to pour his gift of life from this font on this child he has chosen.

BLESSING AND INVOCATION

Now follows the Blessing, and Invocation of God over the baptismal water, of which the following is one form:

Priest: Father, God of mercy, through these waters of baptism you have filled us with new life as your very own children.

All: **Blessed be God.**

Priest: From all who are baptized in water and the Holy Spirit, you have formed one people, united in your Son Jesus Christ.

All: **Blessed be God.**

Priest: You have set us free and filled our hearts with the Spirit of your love, that we may live in your peace.

All: **Blessed be God.**

Priest: You call those who have been baptized to announce the Good news of Jesus Christ to people everywhere.

All: **Blessed be God.**

Priest: (If the water is not already blessed).

You have called your child, N., to this cleansing water and new birth that by sharing the faith of your Church he (she) might have eternal life. Bless ✠ this water in which he (she) will be baptized. We ask this in the name of Christ our Lord.

(If the water is already blessed).

You have called your child N., to this cleansing water that he (she) may share in the faith of your Church and have eternal life. By the mystery of this consecrated water lead him (her) to a new and spiritual birth. Through Christ our Lord.

All: **Amen.**

RENUNCIATION OF SIN & PROFESSION OF FAITH

A renunciation of Sin and Profession of Faith follows next. The Priest addresses the Parents and Godparents:

Priest: Dear parents and godparents:
You have come here to present this child for baptism. By water and the Holy Spirit he (she) is to receive the gift of new life from God, who is love. On your part, you must make it your constant care to bring him (her) up in the practice of the faith. See that the divine life which God gives him (her) is kept safe from the poison of sin, to grow always stronger in his (her) heart.
If your faith makes you ready to accept this responsibility, renew now the vows of your own baptism. Reject sin; profess your faith in Christ Jesus. This is the faith of the Church. This is the faith in which this child is about to be baptized. Do you reject Satan?

Parents & Godparents: **I do.**

Priest: And all his works?
Parents & Godparents: **I do.**

Priest: And all his empty promises?
Parents & Godparents: **I do.**

Priest: Do you believe in God, the Father almighty, creator of heaven and earth?
Parents & Godparents: **I do.**

Priest: Do you believe in Jesus Christ, his only Son, our Lord, who was born of the Virgin Mary, was crucified, died, and was buried, rose from the dead, and is now seated at the right hand of the Father?

Parents & Godparents: **I do.**

Priest: Do you believe in the Holy Spirit, the holy catholic Church, the communion of saints, the forgiveness of sins, the resurrection of the body, and life everlasting?

Parents & Godparents: **I do.**

Priest: This is our faith. This is the faith of the Church. We are proud to profess it, in Christ Jesus our Lord.

All: **Amen.**

BAPTISM

Before the Baptism itself, the Priest asks Parents and Godparents this final question:

Priest: Is it your will that N. should be baptized in the faith of the Church, which we have all professed with you?

Parents & Godparents: **It is.**

The Priest pours water over the child's head three times, saying:

Priest: N., I baptize you in the name of the Father, and of the Son, and of the Holy Spirit.

ANOINTING WITH CHRISM

After Baptism comes the Anointing with Chrism, the Christian's consecration to God. The Priest introduces it as follows:

Priest: God the Father of our Lord Jesus Christ has freed you from sin, given you a new birth by water and the Holy Spirit, and welcomed you into this holy people. He now anoints you with the chrism of salvation. As Christ was anointed Priest, Prophet, and King, so may you live always as a member of his body, sharing everlasting life.

All: **Amen.**

The Priest anoints the child on the crown of the head with the sacred chrism.

CLOTHING WITH A WHITE GARMENT

The Clothing with a White Garment follows: if possible, one provided by the parents or friends. The Priest introduces it as follows:

Priest: N., you have become a new creation, and have clothed yourself in Christ.
See in this white garment the outward sign of your Christian dignity. With your family and friends to help you by word and example, bring that dignity unstained into the everlasting life of heaven.

All: **Amen.**

The white garment is put on the child.

LIGHTED CANDLE

The Giving of the Lighted Candle now follows. Holding the paschal candle, the Priest says:

Priest: Receive the light of Christ.

(a member of the family, e.g. the father or godfather, lights the child's candle from the paschal candle).

Priest: Parents and godparents, this light is entrusted to you to be kept burning brightly. This child of yours has been enlightened by Christ. He (she) is to walk always as a child of the light. May he (she) keep the flame of faith alive in his (her) heart. When the Lord comes, may he (she) go out to meet him with all the saints in the heavenly kingdom.

PRAYERS OVER EARS AND MOUTH

(usually omitted in England and Wales).

The Priest touches the ears and mouth of the child with his thumb, saying:

Priest: The Lord Jesus made the deaf hear and the dumb speak. May he soon touch your ears to receive his word, and your mouth to proclaim his faith, to the praise and glory of God the Father.

All: **Amen.**

PROCESSION

All now proceed to the sanctuary for the Concluding Rite. The lighted candle is carried for the child. A baptismal hymn may be sung.

Conclusion of the Rite

OUR FATHER

As a new member of the Church, the child has a right to take part in the Eucharist, and, when old enough, will receive Holy Communion from the altar, God's table. As a sign of this future event, all say the *Our Father* on behalf of the child. First, the Priest addresses all present:

Priest: My dear brethren, this child has been reborn in baptism. He (she) is now called the child of God, for so indeed he (she) is. In confirmation he (she) will receive the fullness of God's Spirit. In holy communion he (she) will share the banquet of Christ's sacrifice, calling God his (her) Father in the midst of the Church. In the name of this child, in the Spirit of our common sonship, let us pray together in the words our Lord has given us:

All: **Our Father, who art in heaven,**
hallowed be thy name.
Thy kingdom come.
Thy will be done on earth, as it is in heaven.
Give us this day our daily bread,
and forgive us our trespasses,
as we forgive those who trespass against us,
and lead us not into temptation,
but deliver us from evil.

BLESSING

The Priest now blesses the Mother, who holds her child in her arms, then the Father, and lastly the entire Assembly in a form such as the following:

Priest: God the Father, through his Son, the Virgin Mary's child, has brought joy to all Christian mothers, as they see the hope of eternal life shine on their children. May he bless the mother of this child. She now thanks God for the gift of her child. May she be one with him (her) in thanking him for ever in heaven, in Christ Jesus our Lord.

All: **Amen.**

Priest: God is the giver of all life, human and divine. May he bless the father of this child. He and his wife will be the first teachers of their child in the ways of faith. May they be also the best of teachers, bearing witness to the faith by what they say and do in Christ Jesus our Lord.

All: **Amen.**

Priest: By God's gift, through water and the Holy Spirit, we are reborn to everlasting life. In his goodness, may he continue to pour out his blessings upon these sons and daughters of his. May he make them always, wherever they may be, faithful members of his holy people. May he send his peace upon all who are gathered here, in Christ Jesus our Lord.

All: **Amen.**

Priest: May almighty God, the Father, and the Son, ✠ and the Holy Spirit, bless you.

All: **Amen.**

In conclusion all may sing the Magnificat, or any suitable and joyful hymn.

The Rite of Baptism for Several Children

Throughout the ceremony, except where indicated otherwise, each mother (rather than the godparents) holds her child. If the child has a white baptismal garment (shawl), this should be left aside until the appropriate moment in the rite.

Reception of the Children

A suitable hymn or psalm may be sung by the people.

The Priest greets the Parents, Godparents and Friends at the church door (or wherever is customary) and speaks to them of the special joy of this occasion.

He then questions the Parents of each child, in these or similar words:

Priest: What name have you given your child?
The Parents give the child's name.

Priest: What do you ask of God's Church for N.?
Parents: **Baptism.**

The Priest addresses all the Parents together:

Priest: You have asked to have your children baptized. In doing so you are accepting the responsibility of training them in the practice of the faith. It will be your duty to bring them up to keep God's commandments as Christ taught us, by loving God and our neighbour. Do you clearly understand what you are undertaking?

Each family answers in turn:
Parents: **We do.**

The Priest now addresses the Godparents as follows:

Priest: **Are you ready to help these parents in their duty as Christian mothers and fathers?**

Godparents: (all together) **We are.**

The Priest says to the Children:

Priest: **My dear children, the Christian community welcomes you with great joy. In its name I claim you for Christ our Saviour by the sign of his cross. I now trace the cross on your foreheads, and invite your parents (and godparents) to do the same.**

He signs the child on the forehead and invites parents and godparents to do the same.

All now proceed to the place where the Celebration of God's Word will be held. Restless babies may be taken outside during this next part of the ceremony, but the parents and godparents should be present.

Celebration of God's Word

READINGS

One or more gospel passages are read (texts p. 32) to which all listen attentively. These tell us of what God has revealed to us about baptism, and of the new life, a share in God's life, that is to be given to the children. (Text for a fuller Celebration of the Word are given on pp 30-32).

HOMILY

A short Homily or Instruction is now given (at the end of which the Priest may invite those present to pray silently for a short time).

THE BIDDING PRAYER

The Intercessions follow, with these or similar invocations:

Priest: My dear brethren, let us ask our Lord Jesus Christ to look lovingly on these children who are to be baptized, on their parents and godparents, and on all the baptized.

Reader: By the mystery of your death and resurrection, bathe these children in light, give them the new life of baptism and welcome them into your holy Church.
Lord, hear us.

All: **Lord, graciously hear us.**

Reader: Through baptism and confirmation, make them your faithful followers and witnesses to your gospel.
Lord, hear us.

All: **Lord, graciously hear us.**

Reader: Lead them by a holy life to the joys of God's Kingdom.
Lord, hear us.

All: **Lord, graciously hear us.**

Reader: Make the lives of their parents and godparents examples of faith to inspire these children.
Lord, hear us.

All: **Lord, graciously hear us.**

Several Children

Reader:	Keep their families always in your love.
	Lord, hear us.
All:	**Lord, graciously hear us.**

Reader:	Renew the grace of our baptism in each one of us.
	Lord, hear us.
All:	**Lord, graciously hear us.**

Children who were taken out earlier are now brought back again.

INVOCATION OF THE SAINTS

The Priest leads the Invocation of the Saints, as follows:

| Priest: | Holy Mary, Mother of God, |
| All: | **Pray for us.** |

| Priest: | Saint John the Baptist, |
| All: | **Pray for us.** |

| Priest: | Saint Joseph, |
| All: | **Pray for us.** |

| Priest: | Saint Peter and Saint Paul, |
| All: | **Pray for us.** |

| Priest: | Saint N |

He may here add the names of other patron saints, e.g. those of the children, of the church and of the place. To each, the People answer:

| All: | **Pray for us.** |

| Priest: | All holy men and women. |
| All: | **Pray for us.** |

Exorcism and Anointing

PRAYER OF EXORCISM

The Prayer of Exorcism (of which the following is one form), and the Anointing with Oil of Catechumens, prepare the children for the coming of the new life of God in baptism.

Priest: Almighty and ever-living God,
you sent your only Son into the world
to cast out the power of Satan, spirit of evil,
to rescue man from the kingdom of darkness,
and bring him into the splendour of your kingdom
      of light.
We pray for these children:
set them free from original sin,
make them temples of your glory,
and send your Holy Spirit to dwell within them.
Through Christ our Lord.

All: **Amen.**

ANOINTING

Priest: We anoint you with the oil of salvation
in the name of Christ our Saviour:
may he strengthen you
with his power,
who lives and reigns for ever and ever.

All: **Amen.**

The Priest anoints each child on the breast with the Oil of Catechumens, to strengthen it with the power of Christ.

PROCESSION

All now proceed to the baptistery; though if it is visible to all present only the parents and godparents need go there with the children, others remaining in their places.

Celebration of the Sacrament

At the font the Priest reminds the congregation of the wonderful work of God whose plan it is to sanctify man, body and soul, through water. He may use these or similar words:

Priest: My dear brethren, God uses the sacrament of water to give his divine life to those who believe in him. Let us turn to him, and ask him to pour his gift of life from this font on the children he has chosen.

BLESSING AND INVOCATION

Now follows the Blessing, and Invocation of God over the baptismal water, of which the following is one form:

Priest: Father, God of mercy, through these waters of baptism you have filled us with new life as your very own children.

All: **Blessed be God.**

Priest: From all who are baptized in water and the Holy Spirit, you have formed one people, united in your Son Jesus Christ.

All: **Blessed be God.**

Priest: You have set us free and filled our hearts with the spirit of your love, that we may live in your peace.

All: **Blessed be God.**

Priest: You call those who have been baptized to announce the Good News of Jesus Christ to people everywhere.

All: **Blessed be God.**

Priest: (If the water is not already blessed).

You have called your children, N., N., to this cleansing water and new birth that by sharing the faith of your Church they might have eternal life. Bless ✠ this water in which they will be baptized. We ask this in the name of Christ our Lord.

(If the water is already blessed).

You have called your children, N., N., to this cleansing water that they may share in the faith of your Church and have eternal life. By the mystery of this consecrated water lead them to a new and spiritual birth. Through Christ our Lord.

All: **Amen.**

RENUNCIATION OF SIN & PROFESSION OF FAITH

A Renunciation of Sin and Profession of Faith follows next. The Priest addresses the Parents and Godparents:

Priest: Dear parents and godparents:
You have come here to present these children for baptism. By water and the Holy Spirit they are to receive the gift of new life from God, who is love. On your part, you must make it your constant care to bring them up in the practice of the faith. See that the divine life which God gives them is kept safe from the poison of sin, to grow always stronger in their hearts.
If your faith makes you ready to accept this responsibility, renew now the vows of your own baptism. Reject sin; profess your faith in Christ Jesus. This is the faith of the Church. This is the faith in which these children are about to be baptized.

Do you reject Satan?
Parents & Godparents: **I do.**

Priest: And all his works?
Parents & Godparents: **I do.**

Priest: And all his empty promises?
Parents & Godparents: **I do.**

Priest: Do you believe in God, the Father almighty, creator of heaven and earth?
Parents & Godparents: **I do.**

Priest: Do you believe in Jesus Christ, his only Son, our Lord, who was born of the Virgin Mary, was crucified, died, and was buried, rose from the dead, and is now seated at the right hand of the Father?
Parents & Godparents: **I do.**

| Priest: | Do you believe in the Holy Spirit, the holy catholic Church, the communion of saints, the forgiveness of sins, the resurrection of the body, and life everlasting? |

Parents & Godparents: **I do.**

| Priest: | This is our faith. This is the faith of the Church. We are proud to profess it, in Christ Jesus our Lord. |
| *All:* | **Amen.** |

BAPTISM

Before the Baptism of each child the Priest asks its Parents and Godparents:

| Priest: | Is it your will that N. should be baptized in the faith of the Church, which we have all professed with you? |

Parents & Godparents: **It is.**

The Priest pours water over the child's head three times, saying:

| Priest: | N , I baptize you in the name of the Father, and of the Son, and of the Holy Spirit. |

ANOINTING WITH CHRISM

When all the children have been baptized, the Anointing with Chrism, the Christian's consecration to God, takes place. The Priest introduces it as follows:

| Priest: | God the Father of our Lord Jesus Christ has freed you from sin, given you a new birth by water and the Holy Spirit, and welcomed you into this holy people. He now anoints you with the chrism of salvation. As Christ was anointed Priest, Prophet, and King, so may you live always as a member of his body, sharing everlasting life. |
| *All:* | **Amen.** |

The Priest anoints each child on the crown of the head with the sacred chrism.

CLOTHING WITH A WHITE GARMENT

The Clothing with a White Garment follows: if possible, one provided by the parents or friends. The Priest introduces it as follows:

Priest: (N., N.,) you have become a new creation, and have clothed yourselves in Christ.
See in this white garment the outward sign of your Christian dignity. With your family and friends to help you by word and example, bring that dignity unstained into the everlasting life of heaven.

All: **Amen.**

The white garments are put on the children.

LIGHTED CANDLE

The Giving of the Lighted Candle now follows. Holding the paschal candle, the Priest says:

Priest: Receive the light of Christ.

       (a member of each family, e.g. the father or godfather, lights the child's candle from the paschal candle).

Priest: Parents and godparents, this light is entrusted to you to be kept burning brightly. These children of yours have been enlightened by Christ. They are to walk always as children of the light. May they keep the flame of faith alive in their hearts. When the Lord comes, may they go out to meet him with all the saints in the heavenly kingdom.

PRAYERS OVER EARS AND MOUTH

(usually omitted in England and Wales).

The Priest touches the ears and mouth of the child with his thumb, saying:

Priest: The Lord Jesus made the deaf hear and the dumb speak. May he soon touch your ears to receive his word, and your mouth to proclaim his faith, to the praise and glory of God the Father.

All: **Amen.**

PROCESSION

All now proceed to the sanctuary for the Concluding Rite. The lighted candle is carried for each child. A baptismal hymn may be sung.

Conclusion of the Rite

OUR FATHER

As new members of the Church, the children have a right to take part in the Eucharist, and, when old enough, they will receive Holy Communion from the altar, God's table. As a sign of this future event, all say the *Our Father* on behalf of the children. First, the Priest addresses all present:

Priest: My dear brethren, these children have been reborn in baptism. They are now called children of God, for so indeed they are. In confirmation they will receive the fullness of God's Spirit. In holy communion they will share the banquet of Christ's sacrifice, calling God their Father in the midst of the Church. In their name, in the Spirit of our common sonship, let us pray together in the words our Lord has given us:

All: **Our Father, who art in heaven,**
hallowed be thy name.
Thy kingdom come.
Thy will be done on earth, as it is in heaven.
Give us this day our daily bread,
and forgive us our trespasses,
as we forgive those who trespass against us,
and lead us not into temptation,
but deliver us from evil.

BLESSING

The Priest now blesses the Mothers, who holds their children in their arms, then the Fathers, and lastly the entire Assembly in a form such as the following:

Priest: God the Father, through his Son, the Virgin Mary's child, has brought joy to all Christian mothers, as they see the hope of eternal life shine on their children. May he bless the mothers of these children. They now thank God for the gift of their children. May they be one with them in thanking him for ever in heaven, in Christ Jesus our Lord.

All: **Amen.**

Priest: God is the giver of all life, human and divine. May he bless the fathers of these children. With their wives they will be the first teachers of their children in the ways of faith. May they be also the best of teachers, bearing witness to the faith by what they say and do, in Christ Jesus our Lord.

All: **Amen.**

Priest: By God's gift, through water and the Holy Spirit, we are reborn to everlasting life. In his goodness, may he continue to pour out his blessings upon all present, who are his sons and daughters. May he make them always, wherever they may be, faithful members of his holy people. May he send his peace upon all who are gathered here, in Christ Jesus our Lord.

All: **Amen.**

Priest: May almighty God, the Father, and the Son, ✠ and the Holy Spirit, bless you.

All: **Amen.**

In conclusion all may sing the Magnificat, or any suitable and joyful hymn.

Several Children

Celebration of God's Word

(Other suitable readings may be taken from the Lectionary)

READINGS

1. *Romans 6: 3-5 Baptism, a sharing in Christ's death and resurrection.*

You have been taught that when we were baptised in Christ Jesus we were baptised in his death; in other words, when we were baptised we went into the tomb with him and joined him in death, so that as Christ was raised from the dead by the Father's glory, we too might live a new life.

If in union with Christ we have imitated his death, we shall also imitate him in his resurrection.

This is the Word of the Lord.

_____

2. *1 Corinthians 12: 12-13 Baptised in one Spirit to form one body.*

Just as a human body, though it is made up of many parts, is a single unit because all these parts, though many, make up one body, so it is with Christ. In the one Spirit we were all baptised, Jews as well as Greeks, slaves as well as citizens, and one Spirit was given to us all to drink.

This is the Word of the Lord.

_____

3. *1 Peter 2: 4-5; 9-10 A chosen race, a royal Priesthood.*

He is the living stone, rejected by men but chosen by God and precious to him; set yourselves close to him so that you too, the holy priesthood that offers the spiritual sacrifices which Jesus Christ has made acceptable to God, may be living stones making a spiritual house.

But you are a chosen race, a royal priesthood, a consecrated nation, a people set apart to sing the praises of God who called you out of the darkness into his wonderful light. Once you were not a people at all and now you are the People of God; once you were outside the mercy and now you have been given mercy.

This is the Word of the Lord.

RESPONSORIAL PSALM

Reader: The Lord is my shepherd;
there is nothing I shall want.

All: **The Lord is my shepherd;
there is nothing I shall want.**

Reader: The Lord is my shepherd;
there is nothing I shall want.
Fresh and green are the pastures
where he gives me repose.
Near restful waters he leads me,
to revive my drooping spirit.

All: **The Lord is my shepherd;
there is nothing I shall want.**

Reader: He guides me along the right path;
he is true to his name.
If I should walk in the valley of darkness
no evil would I fear.
You are there with your crook and your staff,
with these you give me comfort.

All: **The Lord is my shepherd;
there is nothing I shall want.**

Reader: You have prepared a banquet for me
in the sight of my foes.
My head you have anointed with oil;
my cup is overflowing.

All: **The Lord is my shepherd;
there is nothing I shall want.**

Reader: Surely goodness and kindness shall follow me
all the days of my life.
In the Lord's own house shall I dwell
for ever and ever.

All: **The Lord is my shepherd;
there is nothing I shall want.**

ALLELUIA

**Alleluia, alleluia!
I am the Light of the world says the Lord;
the man who follows me will have the light of life.
Alleluia!**

GOSPEL READINGS

1. *John 3: 1-6 The meeting with Nicodemus*

There was one of the Pharisees called Nicodemus, a leading Jew, who came to Jesus by night and said, 'Rabbi, we know that you are a teacher who comes from God; for no one could perform the signs that you do unless God were with him'. Jesus answered:
'I tell you most solemnly,
unless a man is born from above,
he cannot see the kingdom of God'.
Nicodemus said, 'How can a grown man be born? Can he go back into his mother's womb and be born again?' Jesus replied:
'I tell you most solemnly,
unless a man is born through water and the Spirit,
he cannot enter the kingdom of God:
what is born of the flesh is flesh;
what is born of the Spirit is spirit.'
This is the Gospel of the Lord.

---

2. *Matthew 28: 18-20 The apostles are sent to preach the gospel and to baptize*

Jesus came up and spoke to his disciples. He said, 'All authority in heaven and on earth has been given to me. Go, therefore, make disciples of all the nations; baptize them in the name of the the Father and of the Son and of the Holy Spirit, and teach them to observe all the commands I gave you. And know that I am with you always; yes, to the end of time.'
This is the Gospel of the Lord.

---

3. *Mark 1: 9-11 The baptism of Jesus*

It was at this time that Jesus came from Nazareth in Galilee and was baptised in the Jordan by John. No sooner had he come up out of the water than he saw the heavens torn apart and the Spirit, like a dove, descending on him. And a voice came from heaven, 'You are my Son, the Beloved; my favour rests on you'.
This is the Gospel of the Lord.

---

4. *Mark 10: 13-16 Let the little children come to me*

People were bringing little children to him, for him to touch them. The disciples turned them away, but when Jesus saw this he was indignant and said to them, 'Let the little children come to me; do not stop them; for it is to such as these that the kingdom of God belongs. I tell you solemnly, anyone who does not welcome the kingdom of God like a little child will never enter it.' Then he put his arms round them, laid his hands on them and gave them his blessing.
This is the Gospel of the Lord.

Baptism